LENDING POLICY
IF YOU DAMAGE OR LOSE THIS
WILL BE CHARGED FOR ITS
FAILURE TO PAY COST OF ITS
TRANSCRIPT AND ANY PRIVILEGES

DISCARD

S0-CGP-934

DISCARD

Your Best Foot Forward

Winning Strategies for the Job Interview

Maryann Miller

THE ROSEN PUBLISHING GROUP, INC.

NEW YORK

Published in 1994 by The Rosen Publishing Group, Inc.
29 East 21st Street, New York, NY 10010

Copyright 1994 by The Rosen Publishing Group, Inc.

All rights reserved. No part of this book may be reproduced in any form without permission in writing from the publisher, except by a reviewer.

First Edition

Manufactured in the United States of America

Library of Congress Cataloging-in-Publication Data

Miller, Maryann. 1943–
  Your best foot forward: winning strategies for the job interview / Maryann Miller.
    p.   cm.   (The Life skills library)
    Includes bibliographical references and index.
    ISBN 0-8239-1697-9
    1. Employment—Juvenile literature. [1. Employment Interviewing.
2. Job Hunting.] I. Title II. Series: Life skills library
HF5549.5.I6M55   1994
650.14—dc20
                                                    93–44347
                                                      CIP
                                                      AC

CONTENTS

BEFORE THE INTERVIEW:
WHAT TO DO TO IMPROVE YOUR CHANCES

Marcy was about to give up on the job at the Hallmark store in the mall, when the phone rang.

"Hello, Marcy Smith? This is Francine Bennet at Hallmark. I was just going over your application. I would like to schedule an interview with you."

An interview! What was Marcy going to do? She'd never had an interview before. She didn't know what to say, or how to act.

Marcy's not alone. Facing an interview for the first time can be a little scary. What do you do when you get that phone call? You agree on a time for the interview. At this point, you ask about the company dress code. Then you start preparing.

—

Try your best to make a good first impression even before the interview begins.

5

Pitfalls

During the interview, you have to show that you are
the right person for the job. To do this you have to
make a good impression. When people fail in interviews it may be for the following reasons:

1. Weak personality—they seem to lack self-
   confidence, they are hesitant, and indecisive.
2. Aggression and/or arrogance.
3. Inability to show ambition or interest.
4. Inability to show enthusiasm or initiative.
5. Carelessness in dress and personal appearance.

Prepare Yourself and Practice

By preparing in advance and practicing what to say,
you can overcome the problems listed above.

Before her interview at Hallmark, Marcy should
learn a little about the company. One way she can
do this is by going into a Hallmark store and looking at what they sell, how much things sell for, and
how the merchandise is displayed. Then at the
interview she can talk more intelligently about the
gifts, cards, and other items they sell. She should
also observe how the salesclerks treat customers.
She could get a feel for when to let a customer
browse around the store, and when to offer some
assistance. Then she could say something like, "I see
that you like your customers to feel comfortable in
the store. I'm good at working with people, and
they feel comfortable with me. I feel I would be a
good salesperson."

Using the Library

Another way to find out about a company is through reference books in the library. All kinds of businesses are listed in business reference books. The librarian can help you find the right ones for your purpose. Tell the librarian that you want to do research for an interview.

Suppose you want to work in the mailroom at the General Motors headquarters in Detroit. You'll find General Motors listed in: THOMAS REGISTER OF AMERICAN MANUFACTURERS, which is a multi-volume set, or MOODY'S MANUALS. These books, and other publications, have information about businesses. You can find out how big a corporation is. You can sometimes find out how a company plans to grow in the future. You can also get the names of people in management. It's best to verify these names by calling the company and asking for the correct names. Often, names printed in business reference books are not current.

You can also read magazines about business. These are called trade magazines, and each one is about a specific business, or trade. They can give you an understanding of services and the kind of skills needed for jobs. One example of a trade magazine is "American Printer."

Then when you go for your interview, you can mention some of the things you learned. For instance, "I noticed that your company had strong sales last year. Working for such a stable company really appeals to me."

You should also find out what you can about the job itself. Working in a mailroom requires special skills. You could possibly find out what such a job requires by asking your parents.

Then you have to figure out what talents and experience you have that fit the job.

Selling Yourself

Perhaps you were an office aide in school last year. You may have had to take messages, and pass information on to people. That's similar to some of the work involved in a mailroom and it is good to mention this experience during the interview.

Don't overlook things you have done as a volunteer. Maybe you have helped organize a food drive. Or you and your mother held a garage sale to benefit your soccer team. This shows that you can take on a project and complete it.

Perhaps you want to work as a counselor or in an after-school program at the Y. If you have baby-sitting experience, that will be helpful. Even if you did it as a favor for someone in your family, it counts as experience. It shows that you are responsible. It doesn't matter that you were not paid.

At the interview you will be selling yourself. You want to convince the person interviewing you that you are the best person for the job. To do this well, you have to plan what you are going to say.

—

The more practice you have answering questions and talking about yourself, the more relaxed you will be at the interview.

Planning

Write down the information you want to mention about the company. Also write down your skills and experience. Then practice speaking. You will feel silly at first, but it is important to practice, in order to gain confidence.

You should also think about what questions you might be asked. Then write down some answers and practice saying them.

The most common question at an interview is also the most difficult to answer. "Could you tell me about yourself?" It's hard to answer because it's so general. You need to be prepared, and you need to be specific.

You should plan to tell the interviewer where you live and what school you go to. Be brief about this. Then give your work experience. Say why you want this job. You don't want to simply say you need a job, or that you want to make money. Of course both of these things are true. An interviewer is more impressed with, "I plan to work in business when I graduate from school. Working in the mailroom will give me good experience."

Then you should mention the skills and talents you have that relate to the job you are applying for. If you want to say, "I like meeting people, and have good social skills," think of a specific example.

Write this all out and then rehearse it. Ask a friend to play the part of the interviewer. You might be nervous on the day of the interview and could forget something important if you aren't prepared.

Presenting Your Abilities

Another common question is, "What are your greatest strengths?"

Now is not the time to be shy. You should be able to say, "I'm dependable and responsible. I'm good at math. I have computer experience. I like people and I'm outgoing."

It's important to mention only those things that apply to your abilities. Don't say you are good at math if you aren't. That could cause problems after you are hired.

Working on Strengths

Try to describe at least four or five strengths. To help you find words to describe your strengths, there is a list at the end of this book.

Some people find it hard to talk about their strengths. Some people find it hard to talk about their weaknesses. Interviewers often ask about weaknesses. NEVER say, "Well, I don't really have any weaknesses." You will seem arrogant.

Find a positive way to describe a weakness. "Sometimes I have trouble expressing my thoughts to someone I'm meeting for the first time. But I took a speech class, and now I'm becoming more comfortable when I talk to people."

That answer shows that you are trying to overcome a weakness. Your willingness to do that shows that you have taken the initiative to improve your life skills. That will impress the interviewer.

YOU AREN'T FINISHED YET:
MORE QUESTIONS AND ANSWERS

There are formal and informal interviews. In a formal interview you sit down and talk to a manager in an office. In an informal interview you might just be asked a few questions when you turn in your application. Some managers rely only on the application. Some people have a questionnaire for you to fill out.

An Informal Interview

Paul, who got his first job as a cashier in a grocery store, had an informal interview. The manager called and asked him to come to the store. He asked Paul a couple of questions and then had him

---

Filling out a job application and answering a few brief questions can be considered an informal interview.

fill out a more detailed application. One section of the application was for listing skills that applied to the job he was applying for.

Since Paul had had experience on computers at school and at home, he put that down. He listed that he was an organized person who paid attention to details. He also stressed the leadership positions he had held at school.

"I don't know if that got me the job or not," Paul laughed. "They were pretty desperate for people. So they may have hired me because I was a warm body."

That's good for a laugh, but it isn't the reason Paul was hired. Nobody is so desperate that he or she will hire just anyone. People are looking for specific skills and strengths. They will give preference to someone who can talk about his or her own strengths.

You never know if you will have a formal or informal interview, so always be prepared for both.

A More Formal Interview

When Danielle went to apply for a job at a popular pizza place, she didn't know what to expect. Since she had some interview experience through a class at school, she wasn't caught totally speechless.

The first question the interviewer asked her was, "Have you ever had a job before?"

Danielle didn't think she should simply say no. She hadn't had a regular job before, but she had done temporary office work. So she said, "I've had a few temporary jobs."

"What did you do?" the interviewer asked.

"I worked in an insurance company office. I did filing and copying and answered the phone."

"Okay. Have you ever handled money on the job?"

"Not at that job. But I worked the concession stand at the Fourth of July celebration at the civic center. I did that for four years. I was also responsible for fund-raising projects at school. One of these was the annual car-washing day."

"How do you think you can help this store?" the interviewer asked.

"I work hard and do what has to be done."

Danielle thinks she got the job because she was able to handle the questions. She was able to turn potential negatives into positives. But it also helped that she smiled a lot. The pizza place wanted someone to work at the front counter, so she would be dealing with the public. The manager wanted someone who was cheerful and friendly.

Handling Questions

Sometimes interviewers will ask how much money you expect to make. Most entry level jobs only pay the minimum wage. As people gain experience, they move to better paying jobs. Jobs requiring more skill, pay better. For example, a cashier in a grocery store will make more than a bagger.

If you have a marketable skill you think entitles you to higher wages, you should say so. But if this is an entry level job, don't expect to be offered much above the minimum. Later, you can apply for better jobs.

You might be asked if you are applying for other jobs at this time. If you answer, "No," the interviewer might hold that against you. It shows initiative and seriousness about working if you are applying for several jobs.

What do you say if this is the job you'd really like to have? A good answer would be, "Yes, I've applied for other jobs. But this one really appeals to me."

The interviewer might ask you, "Why should we hire you?"

Selling Your Skills

This is where you can do THE BIG SELL. If you have a specific skill they need, mention it. Perhaps you want to work at a store that sells computers and small electronics. You could say, "Electronics is my hobby so I know a lot about it. This knowledge will make it easier for me to answer questions and help customers."

Here, you can also talk about your greatest strengths. "I am very dependable. When I had a paper route, I never had any complaints."

All work experience is important. It shows that you are ambitious and responsible.

Or you could say, "When I was a baby-sitter for my sister's children, I was never late."

There are some questions you don't have to answer during an interview. It is illegal to ask about your religion, race, where your parents came from, marital status, or age. Most interviewers know not to ask, but some don't. They *are* allowed to ask about your present citizenship, and if you have a work permit, when you are not a U.S. citizen.

You can answer any question you want to. It's always up to you. But you can just say, "That's a personal question. I'd prefer not to answer it." If these questions appear on a form, you can leave the spaces blank.

You should be careful about how much personal information you give out. For example, Paul went to church on Sunday mornings, so he had to ask not to be scheduled for work at that time of day. He simply mentioned that he had other obligations at that time. It was not necessary to say more than that.

Some people end the interview by asking if you have any questions. NEVER say "no." The interviewer might think you aren't really interested in the job.

Questions You Can Ask

An interview isn't just about whether they want to hire you. It is also an opportunity for you to decide if you want to take this job or not. Is this the kind of work you want to do? Are the people you've met, the people you would like to work with? Will this job help you achieve future goals?

If you haven't already talked about the work schedule, now is a good time to do so. Perhaps you need specific days off. You can ask if that would be a problem.

You can also ask who your immediate supervisor will be. It's good to know who will be giving you instructions. You should also know who shouldn't be telling you what to do. You can ask if you should take instructions from a person who is not your supervisor.

Another good question is, "What abilities are you looking for in the person you will hire for this job?"

This question gives you a chance to see if your skills meet their needs. Maybe there is something you forgot to mention earlier. Now you will have a chance to bring it up.

The Choice Is Yours

It also gives you a chance to decide for yourself if you are the right person for the job. Maybe it has requirements you didn't expect, like mopping the floor. Maybe it has requirements you can't meet, like working late on school nights. It's better to know these things before you take the job. Then you won't be doing something you really don't want to. Don't be afraid to open a discussion about anything you want to know.

Common Questions Asked at Interviews

1. Could you tell me about yourself?
2. What are your greatest strengths?
3. What are your weaknesses?
4. How much money do you expect to make?
5. Have you ever had a job before?
6. What special skills do you have?
7. Do you like working with people?
8. Do you want to work full-time or part-time?
9. Can you work weekends?
10. Have you ever handled money on the job?
11. What can you do for me?
12. Are you applying for other jobs?
13. Why should we hire you?
14. Do you have any questions?
15. When can you start?

You should always end by asking, "What should I do next?" Sometimes the interviewer will tell you to call back in a few days.

Sometimes, for example, an interviewer will tell you that he or she will call you in a week. During this time the interviewer will make a decision about whom to hire. If you don't receive a call by the end of that week, then you call. Ask if you have been chosen for the job. This is discussed further in Chapter 6.

The job interview may include a tour of the workplace.

NO EXPERIENCE?
USING YOUR LIFE EXPERIENCE
TO GET STARTED

To get your first job, the hardest obstacle to overcome is the lack of job experience. It seems like everyone wants someone who's worked before. Does that mean you can't get a job? Of course not. This has happened to every person who went out looking for his or her first job.

What you have to do is make the most of other things you've done. Every activity you are involved in gives you some experience you can use to advantage. This is called "life experience." Many people use this experience to show why they would be good employees. Using the suggestions in this chapter, you can prepare a list of skills and talents based on your life experience.

Don't overlook any volunteer work you may have done when discussing your qualifications for a job.

Homework

The information you are going to gather here will help you with more than just job interviews. You can keep it for filling out college applications also.

First make a list of organizations and activities you have been involved in:

- Student Council
- Drama Club
- Youth Group

List everything you can think of. Don't forget church, community, or charity organizations. Next to each organization, write the length of time you were involved, name the leadership position if you held one, and describe what you did.

- Student Council (2 yrs.)—treasurer.
- Drama Club (1 yr.)—handled box office sales and publicity.
- Youth Group (3 yrs.)—organized a softball tournament for last season.

Then write how each position helped you:

- Student Council (2 yrs.)—treasurer—learned how to handle money—shows responsibility, dependability, and trustworthiness.
- Drama Club (1 yr.)—handled box office sales and publicity for spring production—worked under pressure—shows ability to handle details and run a project from start to finish.
- Youth Group (3 yrs.)—organized softball tournament—learned how to schedule events—shows organizational and communication skills, and ability to work with large groups of people.

Next, list awards and commendations. These can be from school, the scouts, a band, or any other organization you have belonged to. Some possibilities are:

- Honor roll
- Speech Tournament Trophy
- Sports Championship
- Perfect Attendance at School

Next to each entry on your list, write the personal strengths it shows:

- Honor roll—shows your ability to learn and excel. It also shows you are a responsible person.
- Speech Tournament Trophy—shows you are able to speak in front of strangers.
- Sports Championship—shows you are a team player and you are willing to work hard for a goal.
- Perfect Attendance—shows you are dependable and likely to be a loyal employee.

Now, how do you use these strengths to convince someone to give you a job?

Working this out in advance will give you a better chance to do well in the interview. Then you won't be hesitant or uncertain while you are talking. You will come across as confident and self-assured.

Let's say you are applying for a job at a restaurant. The fact that you are a team player and work hard is a plus. It also helps to demonstrate that you can handle money. Your speech tournament experience shows that you can talk to customers. Being loyal and dependable is a plus no matter what job you are applying for.

LOOKING GOOD:
MAKING A GOOD FIRST IMPRESSION

Allison dialed Marcy's number in a hurry. "Guess what," she said when Marcy answered. "I've got an interview tomorrow. Can you come over and help me figure out what to wear?" For everyone, dressing correctly for an interview is all-important. It shows respect, and an understanding of the business world.

How you look and act on your interview is as important as what you say. Good grooming shows you are serious about getting the job and that you cared enough to make a special effort. It also shows that you take pride in yourself. The interviewer then recognizes you will take pride in your work.

When dressing for an interview keep in mind that you want to make a good first impression.

Dressing Right

If you are interviewing at an office or a large company, you should look businesslike. A young man should wear a suit and tie. Leave the tie a little loose, then tighten it just before you go in. This way you'll feel more comfortable.

A young woman should, if possible, wear a suit also. Otherwise wear a dress or a skirt and blouse. Avoid bright colors. Don't wear slacks. They are too casual. Also, don't wear a lot of jewelry. Women in business wear very simple jewelry. An uncomplicated necklace and small earrings are best. Rings should be kept to a minimum.

Another Point of View

David didn't think he had to dress up for his interview. After all, if he got the job, he was only going to deliver pizzas. What did it matter?

It mattered because the interviewer's first impression was critical. He didn't have to wear a suit and tie, but it wouldn't be right to go in his jeans and T-shirt. That would say immediately that David didn't care enough about the job to make a special effort.

David thinks that's silly. He believes it shouldn't matter what people wear, and that dressing a certain way doesn't change who they are.

That's true to a point. But the reality of the business world is that people are expected to dress a certain way. If you don't, you will get passed by.

Dress codes vary from business to business, and from town to town.

Nice pants and a shirt with a collar would be good choices for David for his interview. A tie is optional, but it does impress interviewers. If he really wanted to get the job, it would be worth the effort.

Young women can wear pants to interviews for jobs in restaurants and fast-food places. They should be dressier than jeans and should be worn with a blouse.

For her interview Danielle wore black pants, a white blouse and a vest. She wore one long gold chain, a short necklace, and small loop earrings.

One final note—make sure your clothes are clean and pressed and your shoes are polished.

Your Personal Care

Remember when you were a little kid and your mother told you to wash behind your ears? She wasn't just doing it to annoy you. She was preparing you for your future life. You should pay as much attention to personal grooming as you do to what you are wearing.

Most employers prefer that young men be clean shaven. Short hair is preferable, but if your hair is long, pull it away from your face. Make sure your nails are clean.

Young women with long hair should also pull it away from their faces. Use makeup lightly. Avoid very bright colors of nail polish, and make sure your nails are not extra long.

Specific do's and don'ts for the interview:

DO—get to the interview a few minutes early.

DO—greet the interviewer by name.

DO—shake the interviewer's hand if it is offered.

DO—relax and smile.

DO—act businesslike.

DON'T—ramble. Give complete but brief answers.

DON'T—interrupt.

DON'T—chew gum or candy.

DON'T—fiddle with keys, purse, or coins.

DON'T—take notes.

Before you leave home for the interview make sure you have everything in order. Do you have the name of the person you will be seeing? Do you have the address and directions for getting there? Do you have the names, addresses and phone numbers of your references? You might be asked for them.

Okay, now you're ready.

Good luck!

THE MOMENT HAS ARRIVED:
THE INTERVIEW

Here you are, ready to walk through the door. Your palms are sweaty and your heart is racing. Stop and take a few deep breaths, letting them out slowly. It will do wonders for you and help to calm you down. Dry your hands on a tissue or a handkerchief, then let your hands relax. If you clench them, they will get sweaty again.

Then remind yourself that you're not going to meet a monster. It's just one person meeting another person. You're meeting with someone who needs the right person to do a job. You can do that job.

Don't forget to smile.

31

When the interviewer, let's call her Mary, asks you to sit down, take the seat that she offers you. Rest your hands in your lap and wait for the interviewer to begin speaking. Sit up straight and lean forward a little. That tells Mary that you are ready to listen carefully.

The Conversation

Mary might start the interview with a question you prepared for. But she could also surprise you. For unexpected questions use the following guidelines:

1. Relax, take your time, and think.

2. Avoid defensive or challenging answers. That could give Mary the impression you have something to hide.

3. Don't talk about personal problems. Even if Mary seems very friendly, she won't want to hear about your pet's health.

4. Try not to make negative statements that would obviously disqualify you for the job. If Mary asks if you can run a cash register, don't say "no." Instead say, "I work a lot on a computer, so I'm sure it wouldn't take long to learn the cash register."

5. Don't talk too much. Sometimes nervousness makes us rattle on. You want the interview to be a comfortable two-way conversation. Before you go to the interview, practice listening carefully to people. You can do this with your friends.

Watch your body language during an interview. Give the interviewer your complete attention.

During the interview maintain eye contact. Letting your eyes wander could make Mary feel uncomfortable. She might think you have trouble talking to people. Keeping eye contact also shows you are interested.

While you're talking, speak clearly and be careful not to speak too softly. You should also speak politely and correctly. Good grammar is important.

Smile as often as it seems appropriate and be responsive. Don't leave it up to Mary to keep the conversation going. You don't have to wait for her to ask you if you have questions. You can take the initiative.

Recognizing Opportunities

Be alert for opportunities to turn a negative into a positive for yourself. For example, Mary says, "People complain that our young cashiers give them the wrong change." You can respond, "Math has always been my best subject. That won't be a problem with me."

Don't forget to ask for the information you need to help you decide if you would like this job. Ask what date the job starts. Ask what the base pay is and when the reviews and raises are.

If you really want the job, come right out and ask for it. You could say, "This job really interests me, and I'm confident I can do it well."

You could even say, "What else can I do to qualify?"

Most interviews last twenty minutes to a half an hour. That's the talking part. Perhaps you will be shown the workplace. If this happens, it's a pretty good sign that the interviewer is considering you for the job.

When the interview is finished, remember to thank Mary. You could say something like, "Thank you very much. I really enjoyed meeting you and finding out what the job requires."

Mary will probably respond. If she responds, or remains silent, in either case your next statement would be the same.

Say you look forward to hearing from her on Tuesday (or whatever day she said she'd call you).

Smile again, and leave. Keep your head up!

It's over! You survived!

NOW WHAT?
WHAT TO DO AFTER
THE INTERVIEW

Now you can go home and relax. Wrong! Many of you already know how hard it is to find a job. So, if you really want this job, you have to go after it.

Following up is very important. Mary said she would call on Tuesday. But what if she gets busy and can't call? If you call back Monday that shows initiative.

Whenever you call you should be polite and businesslike. Always identify yourself first. You might want to start the conversation this way:

"Hello, this is ——————————. I know you're busy, so I won't take up much of your time. I met with you last ————————— for an interview."

YOUR NAME

DAY OF INTERVIEW

A follow-up call after an interview shows that you are seriously interested in the job.

Pause for a response. If there is none, continue.

"I really appreciate the time you spent with me, and I'm calling to see if there is anything I can add that will help you make a decision."

Perhaps the manager answers, "No, I have enough information."

Don't let the conversation end there. You could say, "That's good. I just want you to know how interested I am in working for ⎯⎯⎯⎯. I think

COMPANY NAME

I have the right skills to do a really good job."

If you don't hear from the manager in another day or two, you can call again. This time you can ask how much longer the job will be open. That shows that you're still interested, but doesn't put any pressure on the manager. Never be pushy.

When making phone calls, always be brief and polite. If the manager tells you they have already chosen someone else, you should still be polite. Don't hang up in frustration or anger. Ask if you can reapply later. Also ask if there was something specific that kept them from hiring you.

Feedback

Getting feedback is important. It helps you prepare better for the next interview. Feedback helps you evaluate what happened during the interview, and helps you figure out if you made any mistakes. Sometimes another person is hired, because he or she got there first. Most of the time, if you do not get the job, it is through no fault of your own.

Don't feel bad. Keep on trying. You will eventually succeed in finding a job.

Paul now has a job as a cashier. Before he got this job, he had applied at an office supply store. He filled out the detailed application and talked briefly with the store manager. A few days later, Paul called back to see about the job. The manager said, "We're not interested in someone like you."

The statement was such a surprise, it didn't occur to Paul to ask what the manager meant. Paul should have said something like, "What is it that made you say that?"

That might have helped Paul prepare better for his next interview. Perhaps it could even have given him a chance to talk his way into the job. Maybe the manager misunderstood something on the appli-cation. Or maybe the interview was too brief and the manager didn't have time to warm up to Paul.

Asking questions is always a good thing to do. You never know when it could turn things around in your favor.

Keeping a Positive Attitude

Going out to get a job isn't easy, especially when it's your first time. It seems like there are fewer jobs than people, and it's easy to get discouraged. But if you let yourself be discouraged it will affect your ability to succeed. Don't let any doubts show. You should appear confident and cheerful and give the impression you are pleasant and easy to work with.

It will help you stay positive if you don't take a job refusal personally. Do all you can for a good interview and if you don't get the job, just remember it's not your fault. Maybe they want someone to work full-time and you can only work part-time. Maybe they want someone with stronger math skills. Maybe another applicant has more experience doing this job.

All these things just happen, and it doesn't take anything away from your abilities. You will find your place to begin working.

Never Give Up

If you do not get the job, don't make the mistake of being so disappointed, you stop looking. The more jobs you try for, the better your chances of success will be. Do something that relaxes you, and cheers you, before each effort.

When you're feeling discouraged, you can talk yourself into feeling positive again. You might use the following statements:

I have a lot to offer people.

I have pride in myself and my accomplishments.

I am a valuable human being.

Being turned down for a job doesn't take away from my worth as a human being.

I am worthy of the respect of others.

I can be a success in all that I do.

—

Not every job is for you. Keep looking and interviewing until you find the right one.

PERSONAL STRENGTHS

Dependability _____

Friendliness _____

Enthusiasm _____

Ability To Get Results _____

Writing Skills _____

Math Skills _____

Computer Skills _____

Thoroughness _____

Common Sense _____

Ability To Be A Team Player _____

Honesty _____

Willingness To Work Hard _____

Ability To Solve Problems _____

Leadership Ability _____

Sensitivity _____

Dedication _____

It may seem very awkward to say these things to yourself at first. It's not something most people are comfortable with. But it is important to keep reminding yourself of your strong points. Never give up looking for opportunities. Don't neglect to look for jobs in less obvious places, such as one-person

Resourcefulness _____

Patience _____

Discipline _____

Speaking Skills _____

Assertiveness _____

Good Grades _____

Outgoing Manner _____

High Energy Level _____

Ethical Conduct _____

Initiative _____

Ambition _____

Confidence _____

Social Poise _____

Ability To Learn Quickly _____

Mature Outlook _____

Flexibility _____

businesses. Look in the yellow pages phone book, and take a chance on just dropping in to visit businesses. Also consider small radio stations. Talk to doormen in office building lobbies. If you keep trying, you will find your first job. Someone who needs help will hire you for your skills.

GLOSSARY

EXPLAINING NEW WORDS

ambition An eager desire to achieve something.

current Up-to-date, happening now.

describe To represent by words.

dress code A set of guidelines about what to wear.

entitle To give a right or claim to.

ethical conduct Behavior based on moral standards.

excel To go beyond in good qualities or deeds; to outdo.

feedback Information that comes back to you as a result of your actions or conversations.

initiate To begin something new.

initiative Self-started activity.

interview A face to face meeting to obtain specific information.

life experience Skills and knowledge you accumulate in your daily life.

mailroom A room or area in a business, where the mail comes in and is prepared for distribution.

Moody's Manuals Reference books and other publications that contain information about corporations and other types of businesses.

multi-volume set Volumes that are divided into parts of the alphabet.

observe To pay attention to; to watch.

opportunity A good chance.

positive Affirmative, without doubt, real.

specific Exact, particular, precise.

strategy An overall plan to achieve your goals.

Thomas Register of American Manufacturers A set of reference books listing manufacturers alphabetically and giving some information about them.

work permit A government document which allows a non-citizen to work legally.

FOR FURTHER READING

Abrams, Kathleen S. *Guide to Careers Without College.* New York: Franklin Watts, 1988.

Allen, Jeffrey G. *How to Turn an Interview into a Job.* New York: Simon & Schuster, 1983.

Arco Editorial Board. *How to Pass Employment Tests,* 7th ed. New York: Arco, 1982.

Bostwisk, Burdette, E. *How to Find the Job You've Always Wanted.* New York: Wiley, 1980.

Figler, Howard E. *The Complete Job-Search Handbook: All the Skills You Need to Get Any Job and Have a Good Time Doing It.* New York: Holt, Rinehart, 1980.

Greenberg, Jan W. *The Teenagers' Guide to the Best Summer Opportunities.* Boston: The Harvard Common Press, 1985.

Jew, Wing, and Tong, Robert. *Janus Job Planner,* 2nd ed. Belmont, CA: Fearon/Janus, 1987.

Kaufman, Phyllis C., and Corrigan, Arnold. *No Nonsense Interviewing: How to Get the Job You Want.* Stamford, CT: Longmeadow Press, 1988.

McFarland, Rhoda. *The World of Work.* New York: The Rosen Publishing Group, Inc., 1993.

Schmidt, Peggy J. *Making It on Your First Job: When You're Young, Inexperienced and Ambitious.* New York: Avon, 1981.

INDEX

About the Author

Maryann Miller has been published in numerous magazines and Dallas newspapers. She has served as editor, columnist, reviewer, and feature writer.

Married for over twenty-nine years, Ms. Miller is the mother of five children. She and her husband live in Omaha, Nebraska.

Photo Credits

Cover: Top left by Dru Nadler; all other photos by Mary Lauzon.
Page 12: Dru Nadler; all other photos by Mary Lauzon.

Design & Production by Blackbirch Graphics, Inc.